Buried Trea...

Liz Miles

Contents

Reema's Journal

5th October

Something brilliant happened today. I got an unexpected parcel from Uncle Globe. Inside the parcel was this journal, a book and a challenge!

Uncle Globe often sends me puzzles to solve. This looks like the best so far!

Reema Trotter
Age 9

Me and my cousin Ruth, with our uncle. We call him 'Globe' because he travels all around the world.

A very muddy field
Staffordshire
England

Dear Reema,

Your poor uncle is up to his knees in mud! Bag-loads of treasure have been found buried here. I'm at the site and we're finding more every day!

I've included a newspaper clipping about the discovery. Do you want to help me solve the mystery of why it was buried? There may be a reward if you do!

Your first challenge is to find out who lived here when the treasure was buried.

Good luck!

Globe

Treasure Trove Found in Staffordshire

A huge **treasure trove** has been found in Staffordshire. It dates from around the seventh century AD.

Professor 'Globe' Trotter

Professor 'Globe' Trotter at the site

Seventh century — that's the same as 600–699AD

I love a challenge so opened the book straight away. First, I'll find out what was happening in Britain around the seventh century.

Invaders!

Roman rule

The Romans invaded and ruled southern parts of Britain for many years, from 43 AD. Most of them left around 410 AD to protect their own city of Rome. Without the Roman army, Britain was open to attack by other invaders.

Violent raiders

New invaders crossed the North Sea, killing and stealing jewellery and gold from **Britons**. These invaders also took people as slaves. In the 500s the invaders (called **Anglo-Saxons**) began to take over and live on the land. Many were farmers.

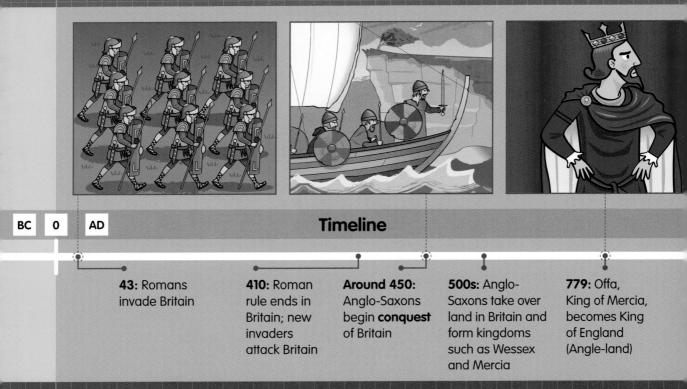

BC	0	AD	Timeline

43: Romans invade Britain

410: Roman rule ends in Britain; new invaders attack Britain

Around 450: Anglo-Saxons begin **conquest** of Britain

500s: Anglo-Saxons take over land in Britain and form kingdoms such as Wessex and Mercia

779: Offa, King of Mercia, becomes King of England (Angle-land)

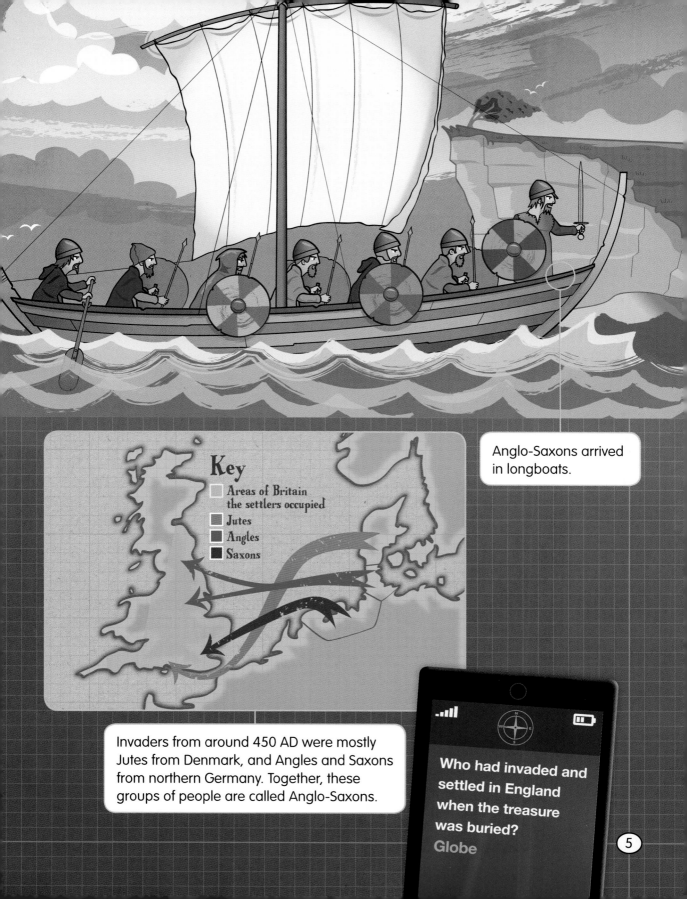

Anglo-Saxons arrived in longboats.

Key
- Areas of Britain the settlers occupied
- Jutes
- Angles
- Saxons

Invaders from around 450 AD were mostly Jutes from Denmark, and Angles and Saxons from northern Germany. Together, these groups of people are called Anglo-Saxons.

Who had invaded and settled in England when the treasure was buried?
Globe

Into Battle

Fighting for land

As the Anglo-Saxon invaders settled, England was split into kingdoms. The leaders (kings) of each Anglo-Saxon kingdom had to win battles to gain land, treasure, and slaves. They also had to defend their land and people from the other kingdoms. Battles between Anglo-Saxon kingdoms were brutal.

Most Anglo-Saxon warriors only had a shield and weapons to protect them – no armour.

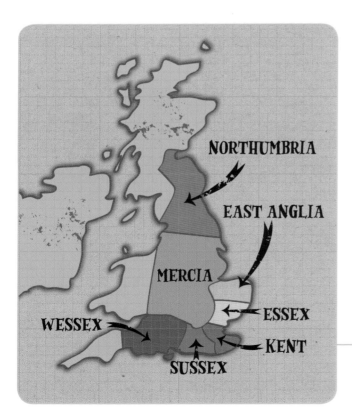

NORTHUMBRIA

EAST ANGLIA

MERCIA

ESSEX

WESSEX

KENT

SUSSEX

Did you know?
Items such as swords were stolen from defeated warriors and kept as **trophies**.

Britain in 650 AD. By 850, the kingdoms of Northumbria, Mercia and Wessex had taken over the others.

King Offa of Mercia

In the 7th century, Northumbria was the most powerful kingdom. In the 8th century Offa, King of Mercia, was such a successful fighter that Mercia became the strongest kingdom. Offa defeated kings from Sussex, East Anglia and Wessex.

Offa built a wide ditch and mound along the border between Mercia and Wales to stop invading armies. You can still see some of the remains of it today. The ditch was:

- 20 metres wide
- 270 kilometres long.

Offa had the first English pennies made. He made sure his face was on them to show he was king.

'X' marks the spot where the treasure was found. Which Anglo-Saxon kingdom would this have been in?

Globe

Anglo-Saxon Homes

Where did they live?

We know about Anglo-Saxon kings and kingdoms from texts written at the time, but there is little evidence today of Anglo-Saxon homes. Anglo-Saxon buildings were usually made from wood so they rotted away.

Looking for evidence

Wood rots quickly so **archaeologists** look for materials like bone, metal and pottery that do not rot as quickly. By looking at the soil, archaeologists can also see where posts, ditches and ovens might have been.

Archaeologists like these dig into the soil to find evidence of Anglo-Saxon wooden buildings.

Yeavering - A Saxon palace?

In the 8th century a monk called Bede wrote about an Anglo-Saxon palace, or villa, in Northumberland. In 1949 an aerial photograph showed signs of a settlement in a field in Yeavering, Northumberland. Archaeologists excavated the site and found evidence of buildings that matched Bede's description.

An aerial photograph like this one showed there may have been a settlement at Yeavering, although it is hard to see today.

The palace site included a large hall, a place for meetings, temple buildings and a cemetery.

Which of the following might survive in an ancient treasure trove?
gold belt buckle
wooden bowl
woollen clothes
silver sword handle
Globe

9

Whose Treasure?

7th October

I'm sure the Anglo-Saxons were living in Staffordshire when the treasure was left. I will tell Globe it was called Mercia. I wonder if he has found any signs of a settlement as well.

I told my cousin Ruth about the challenge. She's helping me. We're both wondering if the treasure is made of gold or silver. I'll email Globe now and see what he thinks.

Treasure found here, in Anglo-Saxon kingdom of Mercia.

Reema

From:	Globetrotter
To:	Reema Trotter
Sent:	12th October 17:28
Subject: Treasure	

Hi Reema,

Good work! The area was called Mercia and it was a very powerful kingdom. That makes me really excited about what we've found.

We've started cleaning the objects – it's going to take a long time though. There are over a thousand items. And guess what? They're nearly all gold or silver and many of them are decorated with garnets. I'm attaching a photo of one of them.

Garnets are dark red jewels

You asked if we have found evidence of a settlement, but we haven't found anything!

We are trying to work out who this treasure belonged to. Have you any ideas?

Globe

P.S. I know you and Ruth love jewels – so your reward might dazzle you!

I can't think what the reward might be. I wonder what Globe meant by 'dazzle'? I'll read on and find out more about the Anglo-Saxons.

The photo Globe sent

Anglo-Saxon Settlements

Living together

Many Anglo-Saxons built groups of wooden houses in the countryside. They cleared woodland so that they could farm the land. Some countryside settlements just had a few small houses. Larger Anglo-Saxon settlements had different sized buildings for the richer and poorer people.

Small homes: Farmers and peasants lived with their families in small houses. The men, women and children shared one room.

Lord's hall: The lord or chief landowner lived in the largest building with his family. In the hall, people gathered to eat and talk. The lord and his family slept in a separate room. A central fire was used for cooking and heat.

Buildings for work: Some buildings were used by craftspeople, e.g. to make fences.

Fields: Sheep were put out to graze in fields.

Fence: A wooden fence helped keep out invaders.

Fields: Wheat and oats were grown in the fields.

Sunken hut: Poor peasants or slaves lived in the smallest homes.

Home facts

● Each house was built from the wood of about 18 trees.
● Most Anglo-Saxons were poor and probably only owned one set of clothes and a few cooking utensils.

Where in an Anglo-Saxon settlement might gold and silver jewellery be found?
Globe

Rich and Powerful

Kings

The most powerful Anglo-Saxons were the kings who ruled over one or more kingdoms, such as Mercia. They were warriors and would lead their soldiers into battle to rob goods and land and to defend their kingdoms.

This helmet was found in a king's grave. It has gold and **garnet** decorations, showing animals and battle scenes.

There are two tiny holes cut into the nose so that the king who wore it could breathe.

Lords

Kingdoms were split into areas called shires. Lords ruled the shires on behalf of their king. The wealthiest lords lived in a large hall, where they held great feasts.

Thanes and churls

Thanes and churls were landowners. Thanes owned at least five hides of land; churls owned less. An Anglo-Saxon 'hide' is thought to have been the amount of land needed to feed one family.

This silver Anglo-Saxon brooch has intricate gold decorations. Only the wealthy could afford gold or silver jewellery like this.

.ıll   ⊞

Which metals do you think were the most treasured by Anglo-Saxons?
Globe

Warriors

Full and part-time fighters

Kings had bodyguard warriors but for big battles many more ordinary people, such as farmers, were expected to fight. They formed a part-time army called the fyrd and were led by their rulers, or thanes.

Spears and shields

Most Anglo-Saxons were armed with just a spear and shield. They stood in rows, shoulder to shoulder, in battle. Some warriors used axes. The fighting was face to face, so it was brutal and dangerous.

A spear with an iron point was thrown or used to jab the enemy.

Shields were made from wood and leather with a central iron bolt.

spear

shield

A typical warrior could not afford to buy a sword.

Magnificent swords

Only kings and thanes could afford to buy a sword. The blades were iron with steel edges. The **hilt** was often carved with good-luck symbols, and studded with jewels. The wealthiest soldiers sometimes had a gold-hilted sword. Swords were often stolen from the enemy after a successful battle.

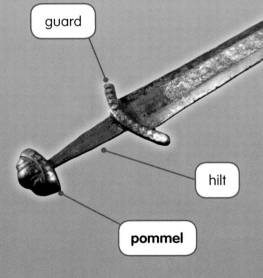

guard

steel edge

hilt

pommel

Did you know?
Anglo-Saxons gave their weapons frightening names, such as 'blood-spiller'.

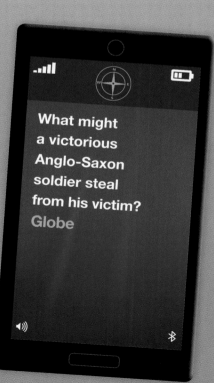

What might a victorious Anglo-Saxon soldier steal from his victim?
Globe

Farmers, Craftspeople and Slaves

Farmers

Most Anglo-Saxons lived a simple but difficult life as farmers. They had to grow their own food and keep animals. There were no schools and the children worked on the land too.

Craftwork

Anglo-Saxon craftspeople had plenty of skills:

Skill	Items made
Woodwork	Pillars, fences, carts, furniture
Metalwork	Metal tools, e.g. iron knives
Spinning wool	Thread
Weaving thread	Clothes
Shaping and firing clay	Pottery, e.g. pots, storage jars
Leather work	Shoes, clothes, bottles
Jewellery making	Glass beads, gold and silver jewellery

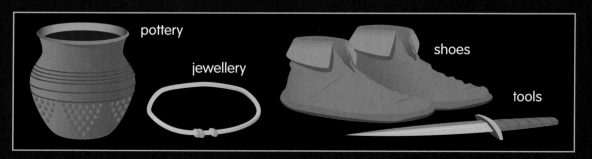

pottery

jewellery

shoes

tools

Slaves

Slaves owned nothing. Some people were born into slavery, others were taken and made to work as slaves after they were defeated in battle. Slaves were not allowed to own weapons.

Most clothes were made from wool.

Did you know?
Gold and silver were brought to England by traders from abroad, so they were expensive.

Which of the different Anglo-Saxons might own something made from gold?
Globe

Getting Closer

18th October

I've just written this note to Globe

Dear Globe

I think we're getting close to solving the mystery.
Ruth thinks the treasure belonged to a lord and lady
but you said there were a lot of objects. I think it
might have been stolen during a battle.

Who do you think is right?

Love from Reema

Anglo-Saxon
lord and lady

Globe wrote back:

Hi Reema and Ruth,

You're doing really well. I think it is probably treasure taken from a battle too, Reema. There are still some puzzles to solve though. Take a look at the newspaper. Any ideas?

Globe

P.S. Have you guessed what your reward will be yet?

Archaeologists still have many questions to answer about their new discovery. They are unsure why the treasure was buried so close to the surface.

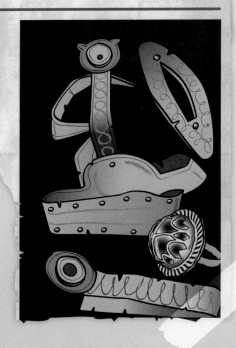

I can't wait to find out about the reward! We're going to read on and try to answer the question.

Treasure Troves

Buried treasure

Although Anglo-Saxons' wooden houses have rotted away, lots of objects have been found in different parts of England. They range from soldiers' swords to women's necklaces, and from **lyres** and helmets to skeletons! Some are found in vast quantities in one place, others are found scattered.

Anglo-Saxon treasure troves in Britain

IRISH SEA

WALES→

DEVON→

CORNWALL

Sutton Hoo, Suffolk

About 20 **burial mounds** containing gold and silver treasures were found. The mounds contained objects such as a decorated helmet, lyre and this golden belt buckle, and weapons including a ceremonial sword, spears and axe.

Wheatley, Oxfordshire

Objects in a woman's grave included a skeleton, brooches and a broken glass pot.

SCOTLAND

NORTH SEA

NORTHUMBRIA

● YORK

● MANCHESTER

● NOTTINGHAM

● LEICESTER

EAST
ANGLIA

MERCIA

Wheatley
Oxfordshire

Sutton Hoo
Suffolk

ESSEX

● LONDON

Farthing Downs
Surry

CANTERBURY ●

SUSSEX

KENT

Crundale
Kent

WESSEX

ENGLISH CHANNEL

Farthing Downs, Surrey

A cemetery was discovered here with over 20 graves. Archaeologists found skeletons in some of them.

Crundale, Kent

This silver sword pommel was found in a man's grave, together with two decorated buckles.

Which of these sites do you think is most similar to the Staffordshire discovery?
Globe

Anglo-Saxon Burials

After death

Anglo-Saxons were either **cremated** or buried after they died.
Pagan Anglo- Saxons believed in a second life, which came after death.

Bodies were buried in graves under the soil. Important
Anglo-Saxons, such as kings, were buried under **barrows** (mounds).
Items were buried with the person, for use in their 'next life'.

After a cremation the ashes were often buried in decorated **urns**.

Grave objects

Personal items in graves tell us a lot about the people who died.
The possessions are often in quite good condition as they have
been buried under the soil.

This is one of the burial
mounds at Sutton Hoo, Suffolk.

A warrior's burial

One of the Anglo-Saxon graves at Sutton Hoo in Suffolk is thought to be a rich warrior's – perhaps Redwald, King of East Anglia. His coffin and possessions were found in a chamber, which was inside a full-size ship under a mound.

The burial chamber was found here.

Did you know?
Another burial site at Sutton Hoo contained the remains of an Anglo-Saxon horse and his rider.

What's different about where the Staffordshire treasure was found?
Globe

Hidden, Lost or Thrown Away?

Hidden

There were no banks or safes in Anglo-Saxon times. People did have keys to their homes (the keys were carved from deer antlers) but raiders could easily break down even a locked wooden door.

Anglo-Saxons fleeing from a raid might hide their treasure under a hedge or in a field and hope to come back for it later. They would need to bury the treasure quickly so that they could get away fast.

Left behind

Anglo-Saxons may also have left objects behind if they did not need or want them any more. An old axe might be thrown away in a field, or a broken pot thrown into a ditch.

Lost

Today, people using **metal detectors** sometimes find a single valuable item, such as a piece of Anglo-Saxon sword or a coin. This may have been dropped and lost by travellers or farm workers.

Items like broken pottery on the site of Anglo-Saxon settlements may be rubbish that was thrown away.

Did you know?

In 2001 a man found an Anglo-Saxon ring worth £10 000 in his garden. Experts think it may have been dropped by a nobleman or woman in the 8th century.

Do you think the Staffordshire treasure was lost or hidden?
Globe

Dazzled

30th October

You'll never believe what happened today. We were reading more about Anglo-Saxons when Globe walked through the door! He was very pleased with what we've found out.

We think that the treasure was buried by fleeing Anglo-Saxon warriors. Globe agreed. We asked him why they hadn't gone back to get it. He thought that they might not have been able to return — perhaps there was a raid or battle. Imagine losing all that treasure!

Globe said it was time we got our reward. It took us ages to get him to tell us about it. We're going to see the real, glittering treasure with Globe tomorrow!

1st November

It was amazing! We saw and touched the treasure — even though it is worth over £3 million!

My favourite piece was a beautiful gold buckle. Ruth loved the sword pieces decorated with garnets, birds and fish.

There was a folded-up gold Christian cross. Globe explained that many Anglo-Saxons became Christians from around AD 597. One treasure was a strip of gold with writing on it which meant: 'rise up, o Lord, and may thy enemies be scattered and those who hate thee be driven from thy face.' I thought it sounded like a soldier's prayer.

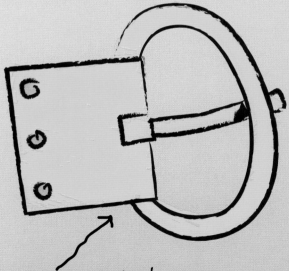

The buckle I touched

Reema's Report

10th November

After our reward I was very busy. I had to present a report on the Staffordshire treasure for school! Here's the beginning of it:

An amazing discovery

On 5 July 2009 Mr Terry Herbert was using a metal detector in a field in Staffordshire when he discovered the biggest hoard of Anglo-Saxon gold ever found! Who had it belonged to? Why was it buried? My uncle set me a challenge to see what I could find out.

Bag-loads of gold!

Archaeologists found lots more treasure in the field – a total of 1 381 items. Nearly all were made from gold or silver and most were from swords.

A trophy hoard?

The hoard was found in the middle of the powerful Anglo-Saxon kingdom of Mercia, which was known for its warriors. There is no evidence of a grave. There were no women's items.

Fit for a king

My guess therefore, is that it was collected for a victorious king. The pieces were probably stolen from defeated warriors after battles. They were trophies of success. Many archaeologists agree with this idea.

Why was it buried?

The Anglo-Saxons did not hide the treasure very deep. Perhaps they hid it in a hurry. Perhaps they were running away from raiders, but then got killed. No one will ever know for sure.

I'll never stop thinking about this unsolved mystery.

Glossary

Anglo-Saxon all the invaders who settled in England in the 5th and 6th centuries

archaeologist person who studies the remains of old buildings or objects left behind from the past

barrow long narrow mound of soil with a dead body and possessions buried inside

Britons people living in Britain when the Anglo-Saxons invaded and settled

burial mound pile of earth inside which bodies are buried

conquest take over land and defeat people

cremated burnt

garnet semi-precious dark red jewel

hilt handle of a sword

lyre stringed musical instrument like a small harp

metal detector gadget that can find metal hidden under the soil

pagan person who believes in many gods rather than one god

pommel weight at the end of a sword hilt, used to balance the sword

treasure trove silver, gold or money that was hidden by an unknown person

trophy prize that celebrates a victory

urn large vase sometimes used for the ashes of a cremated person

Index